The Beats In Words

sareh farshchi

BookLeaf Publishing

India | USA | UK

Made with ❤ on the BookLeaf Publishing Platform
www.bookleafpub.in
www.bookleafpub.com

Dedication

To love

To my dream of publishing my poems

To myself, who persevered through life's struggles and
never gave up, believing in my own potential.
Faith has been my greatest companion.

To my family, who have endured the pain of being apart
and have supported me in pursuing my dreams, even
from a distance. Thank you for having my back.

To my friends, who stood by me through the ups and
downs, offering help and encouragement when I needed
it most.

I love you all.

Preface

I hail from the poetic city of Shiraz, Iran, a place steeped in literary history and home to legendary poets like Hafez and Saadi. Growing up in this environment, my love for poetry was nurtured from a young age. As a child, I was drawn to the rhythmic cadence of verse, and this fascination only deepened during my school years.

A dear friend, who was an accomplished poet, recognized my passion and talent for reciting poetry. She would often entrust me with her beautifully crafted poems to read aloud at school events and poetry nights. Her trust in me and my expressive voice sparked a sense of purpose, but at that time, I never imagined that I would one day write my own poetry.

Life took a dramatic turn when I left my homeland at the age of 21 to pursue higher education in India. The experiences that followed – the joys of love, the pangs of heartbreak, and the struggles of navigating a new world – became the catalysts for my own poetic journey. It was during these transformative years that I began to write my first poems in English, pouring my emotions onto the page.

And so, "The Beats in Words" was born – a collection of poems that chronicles my personal journey, from the depths of my heart to yours. I hope that these words will resonate with you, and that you will find solace in the rhythms and emotions that I have shared.

Acknowledgements

The author would like to acknowledge the poets who illuminate the world with their powerful words, bringing light, love, sunshine, beauty, sorrow, tears, strength, faith, and wisdom. Their work is a constant source of inspiration.

In today's digital age, social media has made it easier to discover talented poets and appreciate their craft. The author is grateful for this platform, which has allowed them to connect with like-minded individuals and explore the beauty of poetry.

longing for the past

I gaze into the distance
lost in memories of those beautiful days
A wish fills my heart
if only I could feel your touch once again
experience the purity of your soul
the warmth of your heart
and be wrapped in your arms
What a feeling that would be!
Perhaps you could take me with you
and show me those breathtaking mountains once more
Maybe in the future
you'll come close again
and take me to those sacred places
Your hand was always trustworthy
I wish you'd pass by again
This time, I promise never to let you go

stay close

You know my heart skips a beat
When the warmth of your body holds me close
Your arms around me
Holding me so close
You take my breath away
My heart skips a beat
Your eyes touch my lips
And I'd hide my real self from you
But desire and affection between us
Hold me back, too close
You take my breath away
My heart skips, skips a beat
I know I'm deeply involved in the fragrance of your love
Stay close, just one night
One sunset, stay close
Be in love, make me yours
Just a dream away
Stay close, one sunset

until

I got all dolled up for your party
I know you're not a lover
you just need a doll to praise with your eyes
You just need a doll to win her heart for a moment, for a
day
You're not a lover and I'm not a doll
I'm not yours until
I see that sparkle of love in your eyes
Until I feel the care in your touch
I'm not a doll and you are not a lover
Until..."

I want her

"Oh, look at her!
She's all about sensation
attraction
desire
tendency
Her eyes are attractive
her lips are tempting
her skin is desirable
Everything about her is seductive and exciting
I want her
Hey boy, please stop for a moment and ask yourself:
Are you in love or just in lust?"

restless lover

When I see your eyes
the shyness in your look
the way you hide your gaze from mine
the movements of your hands
all reveal the desire in you to hold me close
with just a touch, a word, or a stealthy look
I know that if you get closer
it'll be tough for you to let go
tough to say no to your feelings
tough to stop loving the one
who's always there in your dreams and reality
My restless lover
a warm hug in the rain
and a love song would be enough for a while

love

You're pushing me to love
You're holding me close to stay
You're cutting my wings
To shelter me in the cage of love and happiness you've
made for me
And I would call it "heaven"
You're giving me new wings
To soar only in the sky of your love
And I would call it "life"
You're taking me out of my fantasies
To show me a real dream in reality
And I would call it "love"

white flowers

That first day
That afternoon
That long walk towards you
Are etched in my memory
Your smile
your excitement
your energy
your simplicity
and your open heart
the kindness in your eyes
along with the white flowers in your hand
drew me to you without fear
My heart was full of trust and love
Do you know what I want in this life?
To be with you, all of you
And if life were to repeat a thousand times
I'd still choose you, you, and again you

souls

Everything is beautiful
but what could be more beautiful
than the look in your eyes
while the purity of your soul connects
with the purity of mine?!
You've shown me that love is not just about physical
touch
but about the union of two beautiful souls
I see love shining in your gaze
and feel the warmth of intimacy in your words
I'm gifting you a heart full of love
overflowing like rain

rebirth

My heart is beating fast as I dream,
Closing my eyes to block out the world around
My soul is soaring high,
But chains hold me back.
My soul is tearing apart,
Yet my heart still beats fast
My breath is escaping; I don't want to stay
I see a light shining through;
Darkness is fading away
Is there a way to break free?
Suddenly, the chains loosen,
The door opens, and I run away
My heart feels alive again
Love calls to wake me up,
To adore me once again
I see a new beginning,
A rebirth to love again

only you

In your eyes, I find peace
On your lips, calmness reside
your voice is a gentle melody
And your words from a heart full of love
Make me forget the world for a while

Only you , you hear my silence,
Only you know the meaning of standing by,
Not just winning a heart, so true
Only you, you hear my silence

You believe in me and make me believe in love,
You're the one who knows the meaning of love,
Not just wanting a soul, so true
Only you, you hear my silence

sunrise

I'm in love with your eyes,

Don't want to waste a single moment without gazing

into them

I've called out to you with all my heart,

And you've heard me

The sun shone bright,

And I felt the warmth of its rays from your heart

You've made it a pure love,

Not just for the depths of my heart,

But for the entirety of my life

Like the sunrise breaking through the cloudy sky of my

heart,

You illuminate my world, my love

canvas

I feel your heartbeat
the most melodious beat I've ever heard
I'm painting love on the canvas of my heart
with each beat of yours
I'd gift it to you as a canvas of love,
When the stars shine
like lanterns of love around the moon,
my love.

propose day

He proposed
She replied,
"What do you want to hear?
A simple word like 'yes'?
How would you make me feel?
A simple word like 'home'?
Where do you want to take me, dear?
A simple word like 'heaven'
What do you want me to say?
A simple word like 'yes'

But let me tell you the truth
If you're genuine,
If you know the way,
If you understand the world,
If you're a true lover,
If you truly love me,
How could I let you go?
How could I make you feel like I'm not the one?
Which isn't true

Let me tell you the same thing you said:
You complete me,
Like a dream come true"

Mumbai

Birds soar free, souls shine free,
Love envelope us in Mumbai's peaceful breeze
Singing a song, dancing from the heart,
Is this real?

The sky is blue, a kiss so true,
Singing a song, gazing away,
Just at the sun, shining bright
The sun's warmth touches my heart,
Finding a way to say to you,
My love, you're true

love story

A kind look in your eyes,
A deep love in your heart,
Deep thoughts in your words
What can I say about the love I have for you?
Words fall short
My eyes are wet,
My heart belongs to you, always
You're the only poem in my poetry,
The only love in my world,
The only miracle in my story
Stay forever, my love story

our peaceful journey

I'm painting
Our moments
our love
our heartbeats
on stars and moon
day by day
Each morning
I'd open my eyes to the beautiful rhythm of life
sung by birds outside my window
Then my eyes would meet yours
and our hearts would beat as one
Our moments are a peaceful journey
and our hearts know where we're heading
One thing I want you to know:
wherever you go, don't forget my love
You're the only peace in my heart, the only one in my
thoughts.
Hold me close
you say I'm yours
I'm coming from a world that wasn't real

but with you, I find solace
Hold me close
let this breeze of happiness wipe away all those sorrows
hold me close

a seaside evening

in the sea's salty scent, I find echoes of my pain
But when my heart is happy,
It doesn't matter if the sky cries or the sea ignores my
words
All that matters is your hand on my shoulder
And the lovely smile on your lips
The fragrance of love surrounding you
And a kind gaze adoring you
What a beautiful evening spent beside you

shelter

As the drizzle falls, I hold you close in my hug,
Feeling the warmth of your body, tight against mine
I see raindrops on your skin, shining like dew
Breathing you in, again and again, I call you my love

A look, a touch, your eyes...
Oh, let me write, but I can't stop
I'm intoxicated by the poetry of your gaze,
Each time crafting a new verse for the ocean of your
eyes

Peaceful sunset, hopeful sunrise - all reflected in your
eyes
And I'm just a boat, full of faith, floating under the blue
sky of your thoughts
That's heaven - my heaven
Keep the ocean of your eyes calm,
you're the only shelter in my life, my love

valentine

Loving you is the most beautiful poetry in my life
to read
to write
and to adore
over and over again
It's timeless, never fading, and always fresh
Like a gentle breeze that caresses my heart every
morning
it reminds me that a part of me still beats with love
pumping out red blood infused with love
even on our darkest nights

Let's cherish our beautiful
unbreakable bond
untouched by the world
Let's be grateful for it
and live peacefully
pushing away doubts
Our love is eternal
and we're the lucky ones

Love will conquer all
let our souls sing this truth
love will conquer all

You're the meaning of love to my heart
Happy Valentine's Day! My love

two windows

A window to darkness
Filled with ego, hurt, hate and pain
Can you truly find success
While carrying this weight?!!
I still remember
You mocked my dreams
Called them too grand
You urged me to snap out of it
To live in the real world
But let her dream
In her dreams
Love and desire reign
My dreams may be vast
But reality feels confining
Her dreams are Full of hope and faith
A window to light

don't leave

Look into my eyes, what do you see?
Lost in you, somewhere full of love,
Full of you, full of me - lost in you
Look into my eyes, let me adore you
I wish you knew my eyes belong to you,
Searching for you in reality, in dreams, in the future
Hey, please stop, don't leave, look back,
I'm here, right behind you
Let me melt all your sorrows within me
Look into my eyes,
let me live there in your heart forever, my love
Don't close the door,
Let me gaze at you for a moment,
To etch the beauty of your eyes onto my soul
Then leave, if my eyes aren't enough to live for

hey wake up

Lies, and all lies
Your thoughts, my thoughts - all big lies
our hearts are beating, but our brains are full of lies,
filled with empty talks. Stop it
Hey, remember?
you said My smile is your world
paint it on your heart,
Warm it with your touch
My smile is all about love

Hey, wake up, look down,
Your heart is still beating; trust that
The rest are just big lies

murderer

You broke a soul that loved so deeply,
You shattered a dream so pure,
You destroyed a love so true,
You broke me, and in doing so, you broke your own
heart
You tore us apart, and it's unbelievable
What you did to us, unbearable what you did to me
Why did you kill a heart that was still beating?
You murdered a love meant to thrive,
You killed me with your toxic thoughts,
You destroyed a bond that was meant to last forever
You annihilated us with a single word: "ego."

I was a fool, loving you so truly,
A fool for calling you my heart, my love
But in the end, you forgot the loving days
And left me trapped in a cage of love,
surrounded by shattered pieces of my heart
You walked away, leaving me alone with the wreckage
You've murdered a love that was genuine,

Brutally slaughtered our soul
Now, what do you feel? Happiness?
Do you feel at peace? Alive?
No, you won't. You're now a murderer,
Not just of a soul, but of a body, of a love, of us
What do you feel now?

wander heart

Now, you don't have anything in this house,
But you've left your heart behind
Over time,
you'll forget
That you lost your heart somewhere,
A new heart will form,
but it won't be the same,
It'll be cold,
like stone,
devoid of love's flame
You abandoned the real heart,
the one that felt,
Now you'll wander,
with a hollow,
empty shell

faith

And now, here I am,
In a beautiful space,
Looking into myself,
With lots of peace within my soul
Happiness fills my heart,
And I'm alive once again
With no regret in my heart
Because what I gave was only love
Sitting beside my window,
Let the sunrise, sunset, and rain
Wash away all my broken pieces.
The birds are still singing outside,
And I still feel love within my heart.
A sense of gratitude fills me,
Motivating me to continue this beautiful journey
called life
Yes, life is beautiful.
Let your heart beat with hope,
Let your words reach those who need them,
Tell them not to give up.

Faith is the key.
Yes, life is beautiful
Let your heart heal.